Lives and Times

Edwin Binney

The Founder of Crayola Crayons

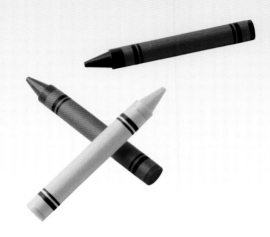

Jennifer Blizin Gillis

Heinemann Library
Chicago, Illinois

Customer Service 888-454-2279
Visit our website at www.heinemannlibrary.com

Designed by Richard Parker and Maverick Design
Photo research by Julie Laffin
Printed and bound in China by South China Printing Company Limited

09 08 07 06 05
10 9 8 7 6 5 4 3 2 1

Library of Congress Cataloging-in-Publication Data
Gillis, Jennifer Blizin, 1950-
    Edwin Binney : the man who brought us crayons in many colors / Jennifer
Blizin Gillis.
        p. cm. -- (Lives and times)
    Includes bibliographical references and index.
    ISBN 1-4034-6346-8 (library binding-hardcover) -- ISBN 1-4034-6360-3 (pbk.)
1. Binney, Edwin--Juvenile literature. 2. Industrialists--United States
--Biography--Juvenile literature. 3. Binney & Smith Co.--Juvenile
literature. 4. Crayons--Juvenile literature. I. Title. II. Series: Lives and times
(Des Plaines, Ill.)
    NC870.G55 2005
    338.7'6174123--dc22

2004021936

Acknowledgments
The author and publishers are grateful to the following for permission to reproduce copyright material:
pp. 4, 5, 17, 23, 26, 27 Photos supplied by, and reproduced with the permission of, Binney & Smith; p. Inc., maker of
Crayola products; p. 6 Alan Schein Photography/Corbis; p. 7 Susan Rosenthal/Corbis; pp. 8, 14 Bettmann/Corbis; pp.
9, 19 Corbis; p. 10 Time Life Pictures/Getty Images; p. 11 Lake County Museum/Corbis; p. 12 Sally Putnam Chapman;
pp. 13, 24 Historical Society of Old Greenwich, CT; pp. 15, 16 Courtney Rushlow Youngs; pp. 18, 22 National Museum
of American History Archives; pp. 20, 21 Sally Putnam Chapman; p. 25 Florida State Archives

Cover photograph supplied by, and reproduced with the permission of, Binney & Smith; p. Inc., maker of
Crayola products

Interior icons Janet Lankford Moran/Heinemann Library

Every effort has been made to contact copyright holders of any material reproduced in this book.
Any omissions will be rectified in subsequent printings if notice is given to the publishers.

The publisher would like to thank Susan Tucker of Binney & Smith, Sally Putnam Chapman (Edwin Binney's great-
granddaughter), and Tad Girdler (Edwin Binney's great-grandson) for their help in the preparation of this book

Some words are shown in bold, **like this**. You can find out what they mean by looking in the glossary.

Contents

A Colorful Man

Edwin Binney did not **invent** crayons—but he did invent better and cheaper crayons. Edwin was good at knowing what people needed, and getting people to work together.

Edwin made Crayola crayons into one of the world's best-known products. In 1998, the United States Post Office made this stamp to honor them.

Crayola Crayons 1903

1998

4

Edwin was a good father. He liked spending time with his family. He was a good boss, too. He treated his workers fairly. He did what he could to make the towns he lived in better.

Edwin (left) is pictured here with his cousin and **business** partner, C. Harold Smith.

Childhood

Edwin was born on November 24, 1866, in Shrub Oak, New York. Edwin's mother was named Annie Conklin. His father, Joseph, was from Great Britain.

This is Bear Mountain Bridge, near where Edwin grew up in Westchester County, New York.

Joseph had a good education. In 1864, he started a **company** called the Peekskill Chemical Works. He made inks, dyes, and paints.

Many barns in New York and Pennsylvania were painted with paint made by Joseph's company.

Early Years

Edwin left school when he was 17 years old, but he did not go to college. He became a traveling **salesperson** for a paint company.

Edwin liked to walk, hunt and fish when he was young.

In the late 1800s, people drilled for oil and natural gas in West Virginia and Pennsylvania.

When he was 19 years old, Edwin started a **natural gas company**. He met with owners of other natural gas companies. They decided to join together to make one company. Edwin was chosen to be the company president.

Two Partners

In 1880 Edwin's father opened an office in New York City. In 1885 he **retired**. Edwin and his cousin, C. Harold Smith, took over the family **business**.

This is how New York looked in 1887.

Edwin and Harold changed the name of the **company** to Binney & Smith. The company started to make different things, like a new kind of black coloring. It was used to make black car tires.

The first cars had white tires. Carmakers soon found that black tires lasted longer than white ones.

Marriage and Family

In the 1880s, Edwin and Harold started to sell school supplies in New York City. In 1886, Edwin married a teacher named Alice Stead. Edwin built a big house in Sound Beach, Connecticut for them to live in.

This old picture shows the Binneys' house, Rocklyn, in Connecticut.

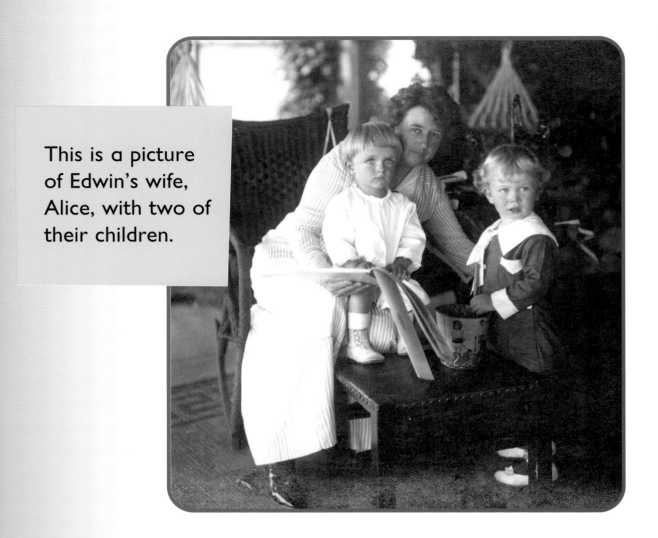

This is a picture
of Edwin's wife,
Alice, with two of
their children.

Edwin and Alice had four children. They
were named Dorothy, Helen, Mary, and
Edwin Jr.. Edwin taught his children to
swim and to sail boats.

Big Business

In 1900 Edwin bought a **mill** in Easton, Pennsylvania. He and his cousin, Harold, began making slate pencils there.

In Edwin's time, school children wrote on slates instead of paper. Slates were like small blackboards that children could hold in their hands.

Schoolteachers did not like the blackboard chalk they had to use. It fell apart and made a lot of dust. Edwin and Harold decided to make a better chalk.

Binney and Smith's chalk was called "An-Du-Septic." This meant that it did not make a lot of dust.

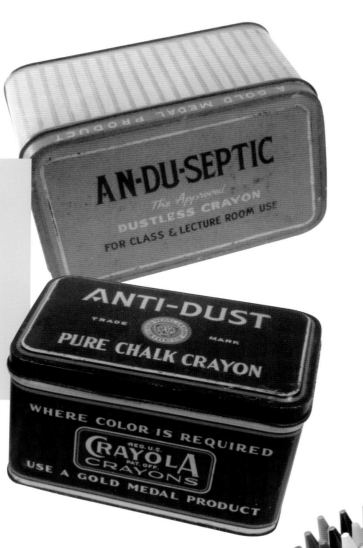

The First Crayons

In the early 1900s, Edwin and Harold's **company invented** a black crayon that did not rub off. They called it the Staonal Carbon Black Wax Crayon. Staonal meant "stay-on-all."

In Edwin's time, things were shipped in wooden boxes. Workers wrote on them with the new black wax crayons to tell people what was inside.

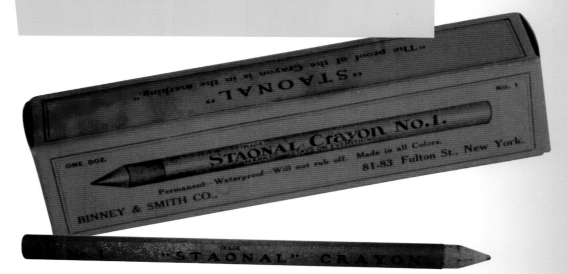

Alice told Edwin that schoolchildren needed good crayons. In those days, children had to draw with lumps of colored clay or chalk. In 1903 Edwin's company invented colored wax crayons that were easier for children to use.

Alice made up the word "Crayola." A box of eight Crayola crayons cost five cents.

TRADE
CRAYOLA
MARK
GOLD MEDAL
EIGHT COLORS
SCHOOL CRAYONS
FOR EDUCATIONAL COLOR WORK.
MANUFACTURED BY
BINNEY & SMITH CO.
NEW YORK. PARIS.

Growing Business

Schools all over the United States began buying Crayola crayons for their students. Soon, Edwin's **company** made boxes of sixteen crayons. These cost ten cents.

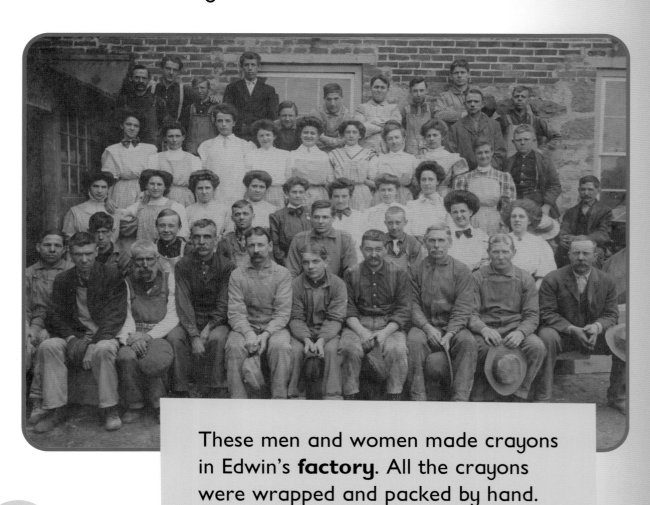

These men and women made crayons in Edwin's **factory**. All the crayons were wrapped and packed by hand.

In 1904 there was a World's Fair in St. Louis, Missouri. People who visited could see new **inventions**. Edwin and Harold's "dustless chalk" won a gold medal for being a good new invention.

Many people saw Crayola crayons for the first time at this World's Fair in St. Louis.

Florida

Edwin and Alice took their family to St. Lucie County, Florida, for vacations. Edwin liked to go fishing and boating on the Indian River. In 1913 he built a winter home in Florida.

This old picture shows Edwin and Alice with their daughter Dorothy and her family in Florida. Alice is in the middle.

In Florida, Edwin had an orange farm. He wanted to sell his oranges to stores. He built a **port** on the Indian River so ships could pick up the fruit.

Edwin worked with other orange farmers to build this port and orange **factory** on the Indian River.

A Good Boss

Edwin and Harold's **factory** in Easton, Pennsylvania, was a popular place to work. Edwin hired people who lived nearby. When their children grew up, they worked at the factory, too.

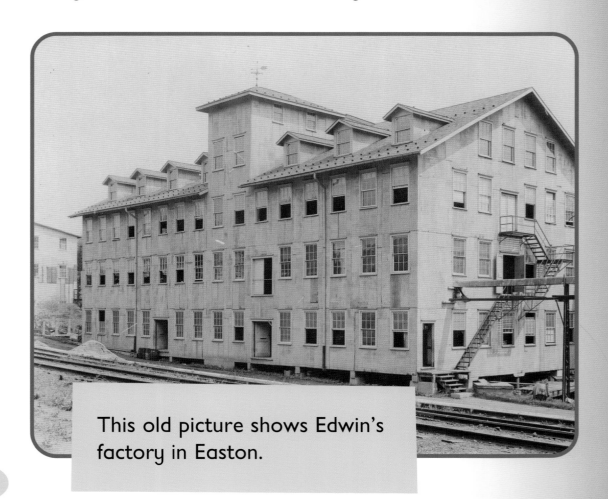

This old picture shows Edwin's factory in Easton.

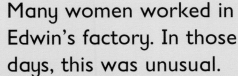
Many women worked in Edwin's factory. In those days, this was unusual.

During the **Great Depression**, many people in the U.S. lost their jobs. Edwin's workers kept their jobs. They worked four days a week instead of five. He also gave farmers work, packing crayons.

Last Years

All his life, Edwin loved gardens. When he was old, he bought some land in Old Greenwich, Connecticut. He hired a gardener to plant trees and flowers. Edwin added a pond and three baseball fields.

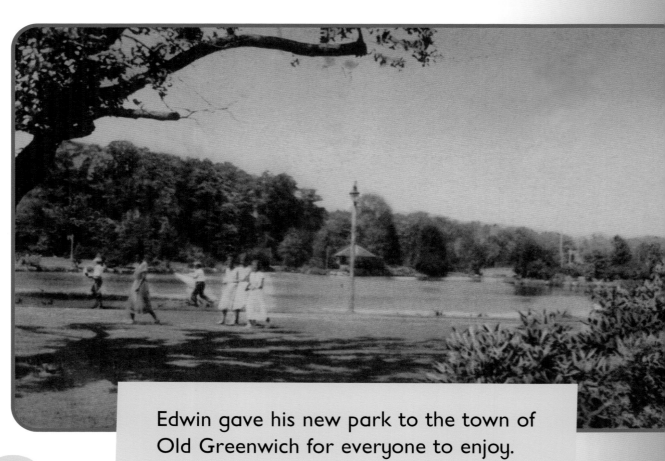

Edwin gave his new park to the town of Old Greenwich for everyone to enjoy.

As Edwin got older, he still liked to travel. In 1927 he and Alice took a trip around the world. In 1934 he visited his grandson in Florida. On the way home, Edwin had a heart attack and died.

Edwin died after visiting his grandson at this college in Gainsville, Florida.

More About Binney & Smith

Crayola crayons are still made the same way. All the colors begin as powders that are heated. Then they are mixed with wax and poured into crayon **molds**.

Mr. Rogers showed children how Crayola crayons were made on his T.V. show.

More than 120 billion Crayola crayons have been sold since 1903. Today, people can visit a museum at the Crayola Factory at Two Rivers Landing in Easton, Pennsylvania.

Children can learn about Crayola products at the Crayola Factory museum.

Fact File

- Three of Edwin's children became very well known. Helen became a member of the **House of Representatives**. Dorothy and Edwin Jr. became champion swimmers.

- The average American child uses more than 700 crayons by the time he or she is ten years old.

- Today there are more than 120 Crayola crayon colors.

- Each year, Binney & Smith makes three billion crayons. This is enough to go around the world six times!

- The most popular crayon color is blue!

Timeline

1866	Edwin Binney is born on November 24
1885	Edwin and his cousin, C. Harold Smith, take over Joseph Binney's **business**
1886	Edwin marries Alice Stead on October 26
1895	Edwin and Alice build Rocklyn, their home in Connecticut
1900	Edwin and Harold open a **factory** in Easton, Pennsylvania
1903	The first Crayola crayons are sold
1913	Edwin builds a winter home on the Indian River in Florida
1921	Edwin builds a **port** on the Indian River
1934	Edwin dies on December 17

Glossary

business activity that earns money

company group of people who make money by selling things

factory building in which things are made

Great Depression time in the 1930s when many businesses and banks failed and lots of people lost their jobs

House of Representatives one part of the government where laws are made

invention something that has never been made before

mill place where machines grind things

mold shaped container that holds liquid. The liquid poured in it dries in the shape of the container.

natural gas gas that is deep in the earth and that can be used to heat houses and cook food

port place where ships can load or unload goods

retire to stop working

salesperson someone who earns money by selling a company's products or services

More Books to Read

Hubbard, Patricia. *My Crayons Talk*. New York, NY: Henry Holt, 1999.

Snyder, Inez. *Wax to Crayons*. Danbury, CT: Children's Press, 2003.

Wood, Samuel G. *Crayons from Start to Finish*. Woodbridge, CT: Blackbirch, 1999.

Index